MY
TRAUMA
IS NOT MY
STORY

DR. ANGIE LESLIE

DEDICATION

To those who seek peace and purpose, may you find your own wings, and soar to new heights, like doves flying toward the horizon.

ACKNOWLEDGMENTS

I am grateful to my husband for his support and encouragement and for always pushing me to be the best version of myself.

To my children, who are always there to support me in all my different endeavors.

To the army of the kings and priests that God is raising all over the world, I say arise and be great.

To my church family and all my spiritual sons and daughters, my prayer is that God will use you and that your purpose in life will be seen to impact others.

Dr. Angie Leslie

TABLE OF CONTENTS

WHEN DOVES FLY

"Oh, I wish I had wings like a dove.
I would fly away and find a place to rest."
(NKJV Psalms 55:6)

Sometimes it is hard to believe that God really does have a plan for our lives. Situations and circumstances have robbed us of our ability to see beyond where we currently are. It often appears as if the forces of nature are against us. It continuously feels like a non-stop battle of one step forward and two steps backward. Yet, God's word tells us there is a plan for us to prosper.

I understand what you are feeling; right now, it would be wonderful to find some peace, escape some of the trauma, and find relief from the persistent pain that has been part of our lives for as long as we can remember. This pain can stem from several sources: rejection, childhood, divorce, the end of a marriage, vision, or goal, and the list goes on. All these things have occurred to rob us of our joy.

We can find little to celebrate when we are enduring the agony of defeat. But there is hope. The Scripture tells us that living a life of defeat is not a part of God's plan for us, His plan includes us living in a place of peace like the dove. When doves fly, they signify the invitation of peace, freedom, and hope to fill our personal space. Doves are often symbols of peace and purity. Their flight can represent the attainment of serenity and liberation. This imagery can be used to symbolize a moment of peace or a new beginning. It is also used in scripture as a metaphor for the Holy Spirit, which is also a symbol of peace.

Happiness, joy, and peace are some of the few things that money can't buy. These things must first be found on the inside before they can be experienced on the outside. They are naturally hard to attain without an addition of grief from trauma on top of it. To truly prosper and embrace a hopeful future so that we can fly like a dove, requires inner healing. You can't soar if you are weighed down by unresolved trauma.

We are all great at cleaning up on the outside but inside, we are like filthy rags. That filthiness eventually spreads to other areas of our life. It impacts our ability to love, have meaningful relationships, successful ministry, and has a negative impact on our future.

God wants us to experience peace like the dove knowing that we are resting in His presence because we have dealt with every negative thought or opinion that we may have had about ourselves. It is not about what others think or feel but it is about our self-perception which causes the most damage to our psyche. When we are free from our own self-doubts then we also are free from others' opinions as well. Through the process of learning to fly, you will discover that God's thoughts toward you matter because He is the one orchestrating your future.

For the purposes of this writing, we will be using a case study to help us learn to fly. We will be examining the life of Adaeze by journeying with her from childhood to adulthood as she struggled to overcome the parental trauma that kept her grounded for most of her life, until God the Father, Son, and the Holy Spirit came along, uncaged her, and set her free to fly. We will see how she went from childhood grief to peace in His presence.

THERE'S HOPE

> *"11 'For I know the plans I have for you,' declares the Lord, 'plans to prosper you and not to harm you, plans to give you hope and a future'."*
> **(Jeremiah29:11)**

After Adaeze had lived a relatively obscured life, now in her late 60s, when most people are thinking about slowing down and moving into retirement, she feels like she is just getting started and is beginning to live her best life.

This was not always the case because she did not have the best childhood. Adaeze grew up in a home with an abusive stepfather who, at times, seemed almost sadistic in his approach to discipline, especially when it came to her mother. The conditions were so bad that all she wanted to do was to escape the madness of a childhood that was void of love and affection which also brought feelings of loneliness and abandonment that were most definitely dominating her life at that time.

The problem with growing up in this type of environment is that you do not learn how to give or receive love because you can only learn these things through demonstration. You can't imitate what you have not seen or known. You grow up trying to imagine what it looks or feels like by looking through the lens of others who seem to have found it. The thought of living a life void of real emotions leaves you drained and depleted and you are left with feelings of being unwanted and unloved.

All you want to do is escape to a place where you feel like you belong. Hence the saying, "Looking for love in all of the wrong places." You are willing to do almost anything to be freed from the bondage that you are facing day in and day out. Having some semblance of peace is better than not having peace at all. Nothing is worse than dreading when it is time to go home, and not knowing what you may find or walk into is the most uncomfortable feeling for a child. It makes you numb to certain situations in order to survive the pain.

Escape meant getting married and pregnant at a young age to have some semblance of control over your life. But those types of decisions bring about another level of hardship because you find yourself trying to operate in roles such as wife and mother that you have not been prepared for. You must now define what that looks like based on your limited understanding of family, whether misguided or not.

Adaeze did not have the luxury of having a role model to follow because her mother was too busy trying to avoid being beaten. She had neither the desire nor the ability to show any love to or teach her daughters how to properly raise a family and take care of a household.

So, for Adaeze, marriage was just a way of escaping. However, reality will eventually catch up, forcing you to deal with it one way or another. Although free from the physical scars of trauma, mental scars still existed. Adaeze faced the difficult choice of whether to acknowledge the trauma and, if so, how to address it.

She felt that she could either take control of her situation or shrivel up and die. Adaeze decided to confront the trauma to get healed from it as she realized the impact that it was having on her life. She felt her life was in a holding pattern; she could not move forward or backward. She always felt there was more to her life. But she couldn't figure out what that something was. The other side of that decision was believing she could do it.

Let's take this ride with Adaeze as she begins to describe her journey to finding peace like a dove in God's presence.

We will look at all the obstacles she had to overcome to finally reach her goals.

CHAPTER ONE

HE IS ALWAYS THERE

"Jesus said to his disciples, 'And surely I am with you always, even to the end of the age'."
(Matthew 28:30)

Adaeze was born in 1958, and just like most people born during that time, she didn't have much but was content with what she had. She lived in Alabama until she was about six years old. Those were the best childhood memories she remembers having. She was surrounded by her paternal family and had the best time running around barefooted with her brother and cousins in the fields and backyard.

Her biological father and mother were divorced and after serving in the army, for a time, her father decided to settle in a different state; an information that Adaeze will find out about later. Since Adaeze was young when her mother and step-father married, he wanted her to believe that he was her biological father, as another form of control, It didn't take long to realize what type of man her mother had married.

Suffering from a lack of education, and no prospect for any real future, the only thing that made her step-father feel like he was in control was bullying and being abusive to anyone and anything that he felt was weaker than he was. Adaeze's mother felt trapped because of being financially dependent on him.

As a means of trying to escape, her mother left her and her brother with their paternal grandmother and secretly moved to NY with the two youngest children; hence the reason why those were the best times for Adaeze; there was so much peace. Over time her mother was able to find a job, get her own apartment, and reunite with Adaeze and her brother. However, this improved condition was short-lived as her step-father somehow found out where they were and forced his way back into their lives. The good times were over after that.

The constant abuse led to her mother disconnecting from everything and everyone. Adaeze never had the opportunity to have a mother to pour into her, groom and develop her, share with and talk with her during those times when most teenage girls needed their mothers the most.

She had to find out about basic womanly functions from other women. There were no conversations about hygiene or how to carry yourself as a young lady. She had to move into adolescence on her own and the first time she fell in love and had her heart broken, she had to go through it by herself. Adaeze became what she saw, lonely, sad, angry, withdrawn, and very unhappy.

As she began to move into adulthood, there were so many mistakes that she made because there were a lot of things that she had never gotten healed from. Adaeze had to learn almost everything on her own and there was so much that she simply was not prepared to handle.

For Adaeze, marriage became an escape, leading her to marry at a young age. With a child and little preparation, she struggled to manage a household and was unprepared to be a wife or mother.

This made her feel trapped. She found herself in a loveless marriage with two children, a situation similar to that of her mother. Instead of physical abuse, it was emotional abuse. She really couldn't relate to love because she never had it. She never grew up in a loving environment. She didn't know what it was like to have a loving relationship with a partner.

It was hard to live through that period of feeling like a failure. However, Adaeze found a way to make it work. The one thing that she knew was that she did not want her children to have the same type of life that she had. She did not want her children to be bullied because they didn't have the latest fashion or to go through life, feeling that they had to do everything on their own. Opening up her heart was difficult, but she did the best she could to share her feelings and to understand theirs.

Since she did not grow up in a stable environment she ensured that her children would not go through the humiliation that she experienced. Her childhood trauma made her a very determined person. She worked very hard to make something out of herself. God favored her to be able to rise in corporate America despite not having a college degree, which she was able to attain later in life.

Her main goal was to prove to herself and others that she was somebody, but it was rooted in outward materialistic things, not from knowing who she was on the inside. The more material things she had, the more successful she appeared to everybody. She even started fooling herself into believing that she was a success because she had the financial resources to buy what she wanted.

Her financial resources may have defined success for her on the outside, but it didn't do anything for her on the inside. On the inside, she still felt disconnected and unfulfilled. She still felt lost and did not feel like a woman that was making strides. So that was how she continued in life, buying materialistically, to show that she had it all together.

She excelled in the corporate world and was finally able to go back to school and get degrees that allowed her to make more money. However, there was still a sense of emptiness on the inside.

As successful as she was in her career, she still did not know who she was. One of the best things that happened to her was that she started going to church and developed a relationship with God. She had attended church before but was never serious about it, but this time as she became an adult and had to deal with thoughts of suicide, because of the emptiness she felt inside, she knew that she needed help, so she turned to the church to seek out that help. Adaeze started seeing the church as the right place for her.

God directed her to a church where their leaders understood the pain she felt in her soul, all the emptiness she felt on the inside. They worked with her, took her through deliverance, she was able to get healing, which put her on a path to finding peace. God stepped in and started showing her the person that she was created to be. She was finally feeling like she could fly.

Adaeze was now motivated in so many ways. A whole new world started opening to her. She discovered that she loved to teach and she began to understand the importance of knowledge. The Bible teaches us that knowledge is power and that people are perishing from the lack of it. Adaeze was determined not to let this be a barrier to achieving her newfound goals and desires.

Now in school, she started with getting degrees in business classes, before moving on to ministry classes. She started attending a local Bible college which opened another world to her. As she began to understand the Scripture, she switched from pursuing degrees in business to pursuing degrees in biblical study, eventually earning her doctorate in ministry.

Through this process, she learned that she was called to ministry. That realization put her on the path to purpose. Adaeze started to understand that God was leading her into the field of Christian education. As God elevated her in ministry, she came to the knowledge and understanding that she was called as an apostle.

She was no longer fighting demons that were trying to have her abort her purpose because of growing up in an abusive household. The Holy Spirit healed her from those feelings of rejection and abandonment. She felt like that dove heading toward the horizon surrounded by God's peace.

The feelings of abandonment were a result of not knowing who her birth father was and why he was never in her life. Adaeze was very young when they divorced, and she had no childhood memories of him. The man that she was living with made her call him father and for all she knew he was her father until she overheard her mother on the phone one day telling someone that he was not.

When she questioned her mom about it, she admitted that he was not. That revelation brought understanding about memories of a woman that she vaguely remembers taking care of her which she found out later was her father's mother, her paternal grandmother.

Adaeze was taken from her grandmother suddenly while she was at work, and she never had a chance to say goodbye or see her again until years later after the truth finally came out. She pressed her mother for more information and got answers about the other side of her family. Adaeze was told that her stepfather would not allow her paternal father to have any contact with her and wanted her to believe that he was her father so that he could have control over her. Once that was revealed, he could no longer control her because she now knew that she had a father who had been looking for her and would come at a moment's notice if needed.

Some years later, the Lord allowed her to reconnect with him, and all her questions were answered. God helped her to find the healing that she needed from that pain. There was now so much peace in her life.

One of her prayers was asking God to give her the heart to love people the way He loves. After getting healed, God gave her a new heart. With that new heart, she was able to love unconditionally. Now she genuinely loves everyone that she meets. As she began to build what the Lord had entrusted to her, she realized that her genuine love was the magnet drawing people to follow her.

Adaeze recognized that she was called to build others, but first, God had to build her. During this process, she had to focus on developing herself by strengthening her character, shaping her future, and crafting her destiny. She approached this growth not from a place of woundedness, but from a foundation of inner peace.

That process began with her philosophy of building with love and purpose. Now, in this season of her life, she has discovered what it is like to fly like a dove. Adaeze enjoys sharing the love of God with everyone she meets and does whatever she can to help other people to receive, build, grow, and walk in a place of peace and serenity to foster their own building mantle in whatever way that God is calling them to do it.

CHAPTER TWO

THERE IS A PLAN

"¹¹ For I know the plans I have for you,' declares the
LORD, 'plans to prosper you and not to harm you,
plans to give you hope and a future'."
(Jeremiah29:11)

As we look back over some of the things that we have struggled with and as we continue this journey of self-identification to find out who we are and who we are called to be, we must learn to acknowledge the role that trauma may have played in trying to abort our purpose, despite the frustrations of feeling "lost," one thing that has never gotten lost is the fact that God still enables us to dream. There is no escaping the fact that when God creates a plan for us, He gives us a purpose, and even though the enemy tries to deflect us from our purpose by instilling feelings of insecurity, stagnation, fear, depression, etc., none of those things stops us from desiring more.

It does not stop us from dreaming about wanting a different life. Despite everything, whether we like it or not, we live in a place of hope. We are secretly hoping that this is not all there is to life and that one day we are going to wake up and magically begin to live a different life. Unfortunately, it does not work like that. God is responsible for manifesting purpose, but we are responsible for positioning ourselves to "birth" that purpose. Purpose just doesn't drop in our laps we all play a role in making it a reality.

The Bible tells us to "study" and not just read to show ourselves approved. In other words, you must go deeper into understanding the stories and the assignment of each of the characters so that you can know how to apply their lessons to your life. The purpose is to learn from their experiences and avoid repeating their mistakes. The Bible has a message for the world, the church, and us as individuals and all of it is waiting to be revealed to those who desire to know its truth.

This is the same with purpose, you must desire to know its truth. You must go after its understanding because the enemy is not going to just let you have it. You must be willing to make the necessary changes to be successful in this next level of life's journey. Sometimes, we will need to be put back on the potter's wheel so that God can reshape and remold us. If you are a little shaky and off balance, you may need to be realigned so that your transition can be smoother.

The enemy understands exactly what it is that we are supposed to be doing. The Scripture tells us that he still has access to heaven and goes back and forth looking for whom he may devour. He is there when God is speaking about you and giving detailed descriptions of what He has created you to do. It is at that point that you become a threat. Satan immediately dispatches one of his soldiers to start attacking to prevent you from receiving the message that the Lord has released the Holy Spirit to give to you.

Self-examination is the beginning of believing that we can live on purpose. When we allow the enemy to control our thoughts then we have given him power to control our destiny. Even though the thoughts and desires to understand our purpose are always present, we don't act on them because of feelings of being unworthy and this becomes a part of our frustration. We feel that we are desiring something that we are not entitled to have because we don't have the right pedigree, background, or circle to birth it.

The thoughts are there because the desire is there. We know that something is missing in our lives and that we are not feeling fulfilled. We are operating out of a place of discontent because we know that there's more to life. There's more to us than what the world has seen. They see what we present, and it is up to us to change the narrative. We control our story and must position ourselves to be our own storytellers because no one can tell the your story better than you. Outside of God, no one else knows you better than yourself.

When we understand that we are not truly living up to our purpose, we need to start asking ourselves why. We need to find out the reasons why we have not emerged as the "superstar" that God has called us to be. Overcoming trauma helps us to change our mindset, belief systems, and thought patterns to start recognizing that we do have the ability to live out God's plans. Once we overcome the stronghold, we can begin to step out into a place of freedom and something inside begins to change.

Our dreams now become reality. We are strengthened to keep moving forward even when the enemy comes to frustrate us. We will not experience a miscarriage of our dreams. Instead, we will carry our purpose to fruition and bring it to life, complete and healthy. That's the plan that God has for all of us. It is in His presence that we find our fullness of joy.

Adaeze got to this place after her deliverance. Childhood trauma made her feel like she was never going to accomplish anything fulfilling in her life. She felt trapped in a life of mediocrity, believing she would never surpass her current circumstances and that too many limitations were imposed on her.

She never imagined she would attain the degrees or influence she has today, nor did she believe people would want to follow her. She recalled a time when she was so afraid to speak that she would barely whisper. Now, she is loud and proud!

Abuse teaches you to make yourself invisible to avoid drawing attention. That's a trauma in and of itself because it keeps you from having a healthy social life. Now her voice is not only heard and respected nationally but internationally.

She has several people that have asked her to mentor them. All these things were a part of the plan that God had for her, it was her assignment. When God says He knows the plans that He has for you, you truly never know what that means until you start walking it out. Once you experience freedom from trauma and deliverance from strongholds, once you are no longer dealing with the hurt, divorce, rejection, pain of parental issues, and sorrow, you can see clearly, and you start seeing yourself in a different light and in a different place.

You start to realize that you are somebody, who has gifts, a calling, and that your life matters. You believe that you have the fortitude to go to school and get multiple degrees. You understand that God has given you the ability to build, create, and launch. You're not going to create like somebody else does, but you're going to do it the way that God has given it to you as it relates to your unique self and your unique calling.

This is such an amazing part of the transformation process. As Adaeze began to walk more and more into knowing these things, the more her confidence grew. The key here is that she had to start taking steps before God caused it to be revealed publicly. There were still obstacles to overcome such as the nervousness of being in front of people, and the fear of releasing things the way that she was seeing and hearing them, but she knew she had to press past those feelings if she wanted to see her purpose fulfilled.

Adaeze had to cultivate that spirit of boldness. That really took a lot for somebody who was accustomed to putting herself in the background. The thing about God is that He walks you into purpose slowly. For Adaeze, first, God awakened the teaching gift and then created opportunities for her to mature in the gift. She started teaching Sunday school, Bible study, and doing some workshops. Then He gave her the desire to want to open her own training center. Adaeze started out training prophets and now she has a Christian University training the gifts of the spirit.

Her ultimate purpose was to birth the university so that people could graduate feeling prepared for their assignment but none of that would have happened if she had not started teaching those Sunday school classes.

Once she knew who she was, and that God had given her the authority to do these things, she moved into a new place of believing. It was a progression that came over time, but she kept moving in it until finally, she got to the place of understanding and manifestation.

Manifestation doesn't happen with a snap of a finger. Manifestation is progressive. It's a little bit at a time and with each step, you conquer a new fear, demon, and obstacle. As you keep climbing, you will eventually get to the place of understanding. Your faith is now at an all-time high. Faith tells you that you're doing God's assignment the way He intended for it to be done. If it's God's assignment, you don't have to worry about the resources, He's going to make sure that you have everything you need.

Regardless of whether the resources needed are financial, people, or something else, trust that God will provide. Once Adaeze realized that it was God's agenda and not her own, her mindset changed. She understood that she had to deal with the trauma of childhood, insecurities, and fears to come to the place of understanding that God is the one who's in charge.

As long as she surrenders to Him and keeps moving, there is no need for her to worry about whether she is going to be successful, or going to be as she saw it in her dreams. Age doesn't matter because it is all in God's hands. He is the one who gives us the ability to dream and causes our dreams to become reality.

God knows the plans that He has for us and since he is the author of those plans, He has a set time for them to come to fulfillment. Adaeze is no longer afraid to dream big because she has found peace in her dreams.

CHAPTER THREE

BEING MADE WHOLE

"When Jesus saw him lying there and learned that he had been in this condition for a long time, he asked him. 'Would thou be made whole?'"
(John 5:6)

As we begin focusing on our dreams, aspirations, and visions that we received from the Lord, we need to assess our readiness to carry them out. Some important questions will need to be answered, such as, "What does my path look like?" "How do I get to my expected end?" and "How do I move past my doubts and fears to realize my dreams?"

To live in a place of wholeness, we must come to a place of admitting that we are struggling with some things. If you can't get to that place of admission, it's going to be impossible to overcome the enemies' deceptions. If you can acknowledge grief, whether it's the loss of a loved one, marriage, self-esteem, etc., you can allow yourself to be healed from the grief.

Acknowledgment is followed by action. It requires some sort of action to be taken to move into a place of peace. Only God can tell you what action needs to be taken and when. Adaeze desired to be totally free to feel good about herself. To achieve that, she was willing to take whatever steps she needed to make that happen.

God was able to do this for Adaeze because she positioned herself for it and the Lord knew she that she was ready for it. You can't experience something that you are not ready to receive. Her trauma is now her testimony. Talking about her childhood used to take her to a dark place, but now she can speak about it freely and use it to help other people to walk in their freedom.

Days after her healing and deliverance, she felt as though she was floating on a cloud because she could not believe she felt that good. You never know how much pain you are in until you no longer experience it. It is at that moment that you realize how sick you really were. Adaeze also realized that there were empty spaces that needed to be filled because the Holy Spirit evicted those things that the enemy used to hold her hostage.

The next step was not to leave any room for the strongholds of grief or trauma to return. It's important to fill those empty spaces with more of the Lord and more of the Holy Spirit. The Lord not only wants you to be made whole, but He also wants you to stay whole. Inner healing is a huge part of the transformation process on the road to recovery. Once you allow the Lord to heal your inner man, then everything else after that can begin to fall into place. Initially, Adaeze struggled with showing love, now she is known for it. A part of her calling is to serve as a spiritual mother to many sons and daughters. How ironic is that! Only God can do that.

The final and one of the most important steps was forgiveness. Forgiveness is a major part of the healing process. Adaeze had to forgive her mom and even her stepfather. She couldn't expect God to forgive her for the mistakes that she made if she was not willing to forgive others. Once she came to that realization, she was able to totally be free from it all and ready to start walking the path of finding her purpose.

Christ desires for us to be to be made whole. Being made whole means getting back everything that you lost. That's the question that Jesus is asking you today, do you desire to be made whole? He's standing by to make you whole so you can be healed in every area of your life and begin to live a fruitful and fulfilling life in his presence.

CHAPTER FOUR

IT'S A HEART THING

"For the Lord sees not as man sees; man looks on the outward appearance, but the Lord looks on the heart." (1 Samuel 16:7b)

In the previous chapter, we talked about how dreams are being held up because of trauma that has not been dealt with. Acceptance is realizing that even though "I'm not okay," I know that the Lord does have a plan for me. The plans will come to life and my dreams will become a reality when I'm ready to live them. God will not force them on us no matter how much we may desire them. He gives us space and room to make our own decisions about when we are ready because there is work that we will need to do to make it a reality.

God's reality is not our reality. God shows us a high-level overview of the plan, but He does not get into the details until we are ready because it is not going to look like what we think. Those thoughts that you have in your mind about your purpose are nowhere near what reality looks like. This is why God waits for us to decide when we are ready to partner with Him for our purpose.

God's purpose requires understanding that He has equipped you and that you have everything that you need inside you. Purpose fulfillment is almost like a work of art. You start out with a blank canvas, and as you submit to God's will, He slowly guides your hand to start painting a picture of what your purpose actually is. Each brush stroke is Him adding another layer of the assignment to the portrait until you finally have a finished project.

Depending on how deep the assignment is, it may take years to complete. Completion depends on your readiness. You may have finished the class, done all the course work, and received a passing grade, however, that doesn't mean that you are ready to walk in the assignment. There is still a level of maturity you need to demonstrate. Each phase of the assignment requires a different level of understanding and insight to be able to move in it. This is why God does not show you the entire picture all at once.

When it comes to implementation, God ensures that your heart is ready for it. Purpose is both a heart and mind thing. They both need to be synced with each other so that you will not easily give up when you are tested by the enemy. God will also test your willingness to see the assignment to the end. Only you know whether it's time to implement what the Lord has been revealing to you about yourself.

Prayer is a strong weapon during this time. Prayer reveals what you're struggling with. If you are praying sincerely and asking God to show you those areas where you need help, then he will do it. Honest prayers, open doors and reveal the truth about us. God will show you where you really are in the transformation process. That revelation may reveal that you don't have it altogether like you think that you do.

As you continue to go through the process of healing, He also will begin to give you strategies on how you need to move forward and start building what you have been called to build. He will also let you know of any additional outside help that you may need. For instance, you may need counseling, inner healing, a mentor, or just to go back to school, whatever it is, the Lord is going to reveal it through prayer.

At this point, your thought process should be on doing whatever it is that you need to do to be able to overcome setbacks to achieve your goals. There are certain things that we're gifted at doing. The Bible tells us that our gifts will make room for us. But it's so much more than just having room to operate in what God has gifted you to do, it's how you operate in your giftings and what kind of lasting impression you leave that's important.

You need to fully commit your heart to make sure that the walk you are about to take aligns with the will of God. If you move into this endeavor just to have a platform then you are doing it for the wrong reasons. Your heart will not be for God or the people, it will be for selfish gain causing a lot of collateral damage along the way,

God does not care how well you package the product; He cares about what's in the packaging and the intent behind the delivery of it. Unresolved trauma will cause you to bleed on the people, whereas healing helps to stop the bleeding. Aligning your heart with the Lord's plan ensures that the people will leave your presence feeling whole and ready to move into their purpose-driven assignment.

CHAPTER FIVE

SEE IT TO COMPLETION

---

*"Being confident of this very thing, that He who
has begun a good work in you will carry it to completion until the day of Christ Jesus."*
(Philippians 1:6)

L ife after transformation is a beautiful thing. Once you have gone through the healing process and are now on the road to recovery, you find yourself ready to move into the actual phase of building. You are at a place where you understand that all the things that you thought mattered and could be potential obstacles are not factors at all.

You see that fulfilling purpose is not tied to factors such as age, marital status, or gender, but it is contingent on our relationship with God. It is a beautiful thing once you have crossed over to a place of contentment. The Apostle Paul said it best, "I learned how to be content in whatever state that I am in" meaning no matter your financial status, you are living a purposeful and fulfilled life because your purpose is tied to God.

It is a wonderful thing to be in the hands of God and watch Him move all the pieces so that you can yell "checkmate." To understand how He works, and how He orchestrates the creation process you must have faith that He will complete the work. Completing your purpose sometimes can feel like this illusive unattainable goal but suddenly out of nowhere, your reality changes, and purpose is now staring you in the face. You are no longer just existing, but you are making moves and strides toward something meaningful.

You are filled with a sense of excitement as God begins the unveiling process. The doors are opening, and you can see your way through. The thing that you were called to do and created to do has now become your new reality. You are excited about the assignment and thrilled about the mission. You are now finding yourself looking for opportunities to share and talk about your transformation.

This is how Adaeze felt after going through her transformation process. After all the heartache and pain, she now starts every day excited about every opportunity to teach, preach, and lead because her purpose is being fulfilled. She is no longer energized by negative energy but by her purpose.

Her days are more focused, and her thoughts are centered on continuing to birth purpose. She is intentional about staying before the Lord to hear what He is saying about her assignment. God is the great architect. He creates the blueprints, plans, and patterns then he shares pieces of them with those who are ready to produce. Production, although may seem difficult for us, is nothing for God. God controls your algorithms. He is the one who places you at the top of the search engine.

God divides up His plan for His kingdom and assigns each of us our portion of the building process. He introduces it to us slowly based on where we are in the acceptance process and our pursuit for growth, He keeps trusting us with more. Our natural limitations do not concern God because they are just temporary gaps. As we allow him to continue refining us, He closes those gaps throughout the transformation process until we become the vessel that we were intended to be at the point of our creation.

Everything that God creates is good and it is marvelous in his sight. He takes great pride when he looks at us and sees the original finished product, operating as intended. Adaeze understands that the Lord is going to keep her until her assignment is done. She also understands that it is not up to her to bring it to completion. We do, however, have things that we need to do in the completion process as well.

Adaeze also knows that she must be mindful of how she treats her assignment and understands that there are things that she will need to guard herself against. Old habits and ways are just waiting to creep back in if she is not careful. She can never let her guard down by thinking that she has arrived because it is at that moment that the enemy will start to rear its ugly head, unleashing the spirit of pride. The completion part of the transformation is such a rewarding feeling that it is hard to put into words, but we have to always remember that we are not the ones doing it, it is God doing it through us.

Every day is a day of accomplishment, whether big or small. If at the end of the day, you can check a task off your list, then you had a great day. For Adaeze, she is seeing her accomplishments in ways that she never thought possible. Writing a book was a huge accomplishment. If being able to tell her story was all she accomplished, that in and of itself would have been more than enough.

The completion process is about getting to the other side. It is about coming out of the wilderness and entering your promised land. Adaeze would say that the 40 years of wandering was worth the wait. Words cannot describe what it feels like to be on the other side of the river, to be transformed into who you were supposed to be. On the seventh day, God completed His work, He completed laying the foundation of the world, and He completed us, not according to the world's standards but according to His standards.

God's completion process is final and set in stone. God named you and said who you were and what you were going to be. It is time to start loving this newfound person and declaring that you wouldn't trade your journey for the world, because everything that you experienced is now being applied, and is part of your walk into purpose.

The completion process involves being able to tell your story without it taking you to a dark place. Your story can become your testimony and you can share it as a testament of what God desires to do for us all. Just as He healed Adaeze, He will heal you. He is just waiting for you to take that first step, and He will do the rest.

Are you ready to be made whole? Are you ready to begin your transformation process? Are you ready to be put back on the potter's wheel, to be reshaped and remolded to complete your purpose process?

The book of Genesis tells us that everything that the Lord created is good, it was for a purpose and for a reason. That is God's message to you today. It gave him great pleasure to create and fashion you in His image, to breathe His breath in you to give your life. He desires that you live the life that he created you to live. There is so much for you to do. Your purpose is for this moment and time. It is your Kairos moment!

CHAPTER SIX

ROMANS ROAD TO TRANSFORMATION

"If you confess with your mouth the Lord and believe in your heart that God raised Him from the dead, you will be saved." (Romans 10:9)

The transformation process is about living a fulfilled life. When we talk about "living in your purpose," we are simply referring to living a life guided by a sense of meaning, direction, and fulfillment derived from aligning one's actions, values, and goals with a deeper sense of purpose or calling.

This involves consciously making choices and taking actions that contribute to a sense of fulfillment and satisfaction in various aspects of life, such as career, relationships, and personal growth. The road to transformation focuses on your personal development.

The philosophy of personal development building emphasizes continuous growth, self-improvement, and building upon one's strengths and skills to reach one's full potential. It involves setting goals, cultivating positive habits, learning from experiences, and constantly evolving to become the best version of yourself.

Unresolved trauma hinders this growth process by leaving us in a weakened state and believing that there is no other version of ourselves than the one that we are seeing now.

Five common struggles that people face when it comes to achieving personal fulfillment are:

1. Self-doubt and lack of confidence in their abilities or worth
2. Uncertainty about their goals, passions, or life purpose
3. External pressures or societal expectations conflicting with their authentic desires
4. Difficulty in finding a balance between personal and professional responsibilities
5. Past traumas or limiting beliefs that hinder personal growth and fulfillment

Just as salvation is available to everyone, so is a life of personal fulfillment, regardless of your background or pedigree. Solidifying your relationship with God is the beginning of that transformation process. The enemy desires to keep us in a place where we are constantly denying our identity. Right now, the adversary has the body of Christ in a state of confusion causing the church to suffer from an identity crisis.

An identity crisis refers to a period of uncertainty and confusion about one's sense of self, often involving questioning one's values, beliefs, or personal identity. We counteract these attacks by being determined to discover our identity in Christ. Romans 9 tells us that transformation starts with confession. We must say what we believe. By doing so, we are putting the enemy on notice that your thought patterns are no longer controlled by him. You are publicly announcing that you know who you are, and more importantly, who your identity is tied to.

Self-discovery is the process of learning about oneself and exploring one's identity, values, interests, and capabilities. It often involves introspection, reflection, and personal growth. Once you **accept** who you are in Christ, then you must **believe** it, finally allowing the Lord to **complete** the work that He began in you.

Adaeze likes to call this process the ABCs of Personal Fulfillment. Some of the benefits of personal fulfillment are:

1. Increased self-awareness and clarity about personal goals and values
2. Improved confidence and self-esteem
3. Development of effective strategies for overcoming obstacles and achieving goals
4. Enhanced resilience and ability to cope with challenges

5. Greater satisfaction and fulfillment in various aspects of life, such as career, relationships, and personal growth
6. Increased sense of purpose and direction
7. Improved overall well-being and life satisfaction

A change of mindset is not always an easy thing to do. For Adaeze she had to be intentional about discovering who she was really meant to be. Luckily, God placed some great mentors in her life who were very instrumental in helping to guide her into her promised land. Those folks gave her the guidance that she didn't get growing up.

For the process to be successful, you must be teachable and have a desire to move forward. It also requires work. It is not a process that anyone should take lightly or walk into if you are not fully ready to put in the work. The acceptance phase requires unraveling years of misguided thinking, from erroneous teaching in some cases, to effectively achieve a mindset change.

Transformation brings you onto the battlefield with the enemy every time he tries to bring you back into that dark place. His job is to continue to plant seeds of doubt that is why you must believe that the person you are seeing now is really the person that you were meant to be and as God completes the process of restoration, purpose is now yours to claim.

Not only can you claim purpose, but you can live in purpose.

YOU HAVE BEEN CHOSEN

"But you are a chosen people, a royal priesthood, a holy nation, God's special possession, that you may declare the praises of him who called you out of darkness into his wonderful light." (1 Peter 2:9)

The story of Adaeze is about overcoming adversities, traumas, setbacks, and disappointments to get to a place of understanding that her trauma is not her story. It's about understanding that no matter the trauma, she was still chosen. Adaeze was given her name by one of the leaders of the IGBO tribe in Nigeria. He told her that God said to give her that name because it means the "First daughter of the King".

He went on to tell her that the first daughter has access to everything that the father has and is the one with all the power and authority. All the other daughters submit to her. That was God's way of telling Adaeze that she was favored and that he had given her the authority to govern and lead.

Adaeze is purposeful in everything that she does now. She is no longer defined by her past but is letting her present dictate who she is. Her current experiences have led her to recognize that her own struggles have inspired her to help others overcome their traumas and discover their own purposes. Her story is about journeying to find what it means to fly like a dove. It means answering such questions as "What does it mean to release your passions, to accomplish your goals, to feel a sense of pride and accomplishment?"

Her purpose is to help those assigned to her deal with their feelings of isolation and serve as a support system as they travel on their journey to fulfillment. Adaeze understands those feelings all too well. Her trauma is something that she had to deal with, but it is not her story. It may have a small piece in her story, but it is not what defines her as a person.

Sometimes, we start to feel as though we have missed life, that we have let it pass us by and it is now too late. The opposite is really the truth. Adaeze began a journey of finding out who she was after her kids were grown and on their own. She was no longer the soccer mom. So now who was she? She still had a youthful presence, she still felt vibrant, she just never felt like she ever tapped into her inner self. But she refused to believe that it was over for her. She refused to believe there was no more purpose to her life.

There was a moment when as God was speaking, Adaze started looking at herself and saying that she couldn't do it, she was too old, past her prime, and she had missed her moment and mark. God showed her how Moses was 80 when he started his ministry. She looked at some other folks in the Bible whom God had called but didn't begin their work until later in life. For God, there is no such thing as being too old or too young, or being out of season or out of time, everything starts when it is supposed to start. Adaeze learned that she was right "on time."

God already knows the moment in which acceptance will take place. He knows at what moment the shift will take place and when realignment will come to bring you into the right place for purpose to kick into gear.

Adaeze no longer feels that she is living a limitless life but that she is now living a fulfilling and contented life. God wants us to know that type of life can start at any moment, as long as you have breath in your body, it is never too late. God knows the time in which that awakening is going to happen. God doesn't see time the way we see it. His ways are not our ways, and His thoughts are not our thoughts. He stands ready to awaken our purpose whenever we make the decision that we are ready.

He will awaken every area at the right time. God is the only person that can fast-track destiny. He will take you to where you are supposed to be by the time you reach a particular place in life. God is not concerned with time; He is only concerned with the heart. There is no wasted time with God. You never need to feel like you missed the mark. If you believe, then you can receive.

Adaeze started believing and is still going strong and conquering the world. She feels that she is just getting started living her best life. Guess what? The same is what lies ahead for you. Just go with it!

Adaeze is grateful that God allowed her the time and space to figure out who she was. She is most thankful for the time to learn how to live in peace while getting healed

Presently, Adaeze finds herself in a place where she has learned to define herself according to God's standards. Through God's showering of his love on her, she finally knows how to shower love on others. The transformation process made her learn some things about herself. The most important thing she discovered is that she is stronger than she realized. Adaeze desires for others to reach their destiny much quicker than it took her to get there. She is thankful for every opportunity that the Lord creates for her to help others experience their own feelings of self-fulfillment.

If you are reading this book, then that means this is your moment. It is time to move past everything that may have been hindering you from your past and press on toward everything that is waiting for you in your future.

God has chosen you for this!

TRANSFORMATION PRAYER

Lord, I come before you with a heart of thanksgiving. I am always grateful to you for my transformation process. You deemed it not robbery, to wait until I got to the place where my mindset agreed with you, and I was ready to be transformed. Thank you Lord for transforming me in this moment. Even during this stage of my life, age is not a factor for your transforming power to be effective. You are transforming me to be even greater and more powerful, more skillful, and more purposeful than everything I've ever known or imagined.

Lord, I will always be grateful because my living has not been in vain. I know that there is purpose for my life. I can look back and see the various accomplishments that you have allowed me to make. I can see the accomplishments made toward the building of your kingdom. I believe as I pray that heaven is pleased with my acceptance of myself as you have created me. Lord, I thank you for transforming my mind, heart, and belief systems. I am conscientiously moving to a place where there's an alignment with your will.

My ears are inclined to hear what heaven is speaking as it relates to the continuation of my transformation process as you continue to grow me, stretch me, and move me into the place that you called me.

You created me in your mind before the foundation of the world. You taught me how to lay the proper foundation for the ministry that you have given me.

I thank You for not leaving me in that dark place where the world took me, but you brought me into your marvelous light, and you transformed me into this wonderful, beautiful creature that I am today.

You created me in your image, breathed your breath in me, and gave me life. Today, I dedicate this life that you gave back to you.

I understand now that praise is a weapon, and I will use it with authority to ensure that every day I'm praising you for the victory of surviving another day as I am learning to live in my purpose.

Again, thank You for renewing my mind and cleansing my thoughts so that I can see and hear your will for my life.

I'll forever love you.

In Jesus' name I pray, Amen.

CONTACT INFORMATION

Please be sure to check out our blog at sparkaca.org.

Visit us at drangieleslie.om for other books by the author and for more details regarding our monthly group mentorship program: *My Thoughts Matter*

We invite you to check out the guidebook: *My Thoughts Matter to get on the road to having a sound Mind.*

You can also purchase the workbook: *ABC's of Personal Fulfillment* as a supplement to this book to get on the road to personal fulfillment.

EPILOGUE

Have you ever felt lost and alone? Were you ignored, abandoned, or isolated as a child? Do you have feelings of living without purpose or direction? Has your heart been damaged by people that you loved?

Trauma affects our lives in so many ways. It creates a perception and feelings of unworthiness. It could leave you feeling unloved and unwanted. The pain leaves us feeling vulnerable, which causes us to become defensive and withdrawn.

My Trauma is Not My Story is a book about understanding the importance of getting healed from trauma so that your mind is clear to make healthy decisions. The enemy desires to keep you bound, but God desires for you to be free so that you can walk in purpose.

God wants to see you flying like a dove!

ABOUT THE AUTHOR

Dr. Angie Leslie is the founder and CEO of Antioch-Global, a private non-profit Christian organization focused on discipleship training and leadership development. Dr. Angie is a commissioned Apostle and serves as an Apostolic leader for the Kingdom of God. She defines herself as a businesswoman, thought leader, and pattern maker providing a blueprint for developing the next generation of leaders across the globe. Her mandate is to build mission-minded leaders to be impactful and influential in ministry as well as in the marketplace